AFRICA

ZEBRAS

By Melissa Cole
Photographs by Tom and Pat Leeson

BLACKBIRCH®
PRESS

THOMSON

San Diego • Detroit • New York • San Francisco • Cleveland • New Haven, Conn. • Waterville, Maine • London • Munich

THOMSON
★
GALE

For more information, contact
The Gale Group, Inc.
27500 Drake Rd.
Farmington Hills, MI 48331-3535
Or you can visit our Internet site at http://www.gale.com

Photo Credits: Cover and all photos © Tom and Pat Leeson Nature Wildlife Photography; back cover, page 17 © CORBIS

LIBRARY OF CONGRESS CATALOGING-IN-PUBLICATION DATA

Cole, Melissa S.
  Zebras / by Melissa S. Cole.
      p. cm. — (Wild Africa series)
Summary: Examines the life of the zebra, pointing out differences
between the three species and the impact humans have had, and continue
to have, on these African mammals.
Includes bibliographical references (p. 24).
  ISBN 1-56711-636-1 (hardback)
  1. Zebras—Juvenile literature. [1. Zebras. 2. Endangered species.]
I. Title.
  QL737.U62 C65 2003
  599.665'7—dc21   2002006270

Printed in China
10 9 8 7 6 5 4 3 2 1

Contents

Introduction

Zebras are closely related to horses and donkeys. They all belong to the animal group Equus, which means "horse" in Latin. In the African Swahili language, the words for zebra are *punda milia*, or "striped donkey." Though the three animals are similar, zebras are different from horses and donkeys. Zebras have black and white stripes on their bodies.

Three different types of zebras live in Africa: plains zebras, Grevy's zebras, and mountain zebras. They are not directly related to each other, and they do not breed outside of their own species. The most common species are the plains zebras, also known as Burchell's zebras. More than a half million plains zebras live on the grassy savannas of eastern and southern Africa.

Opposite: Zebras are closely related to horses and donkeys. **Below:** There are about half a million Burchell's zebras in Africa.

The Body of a Zebra

Zebras look like small horses with striped coats. They have thick bodies, muscular legs, and powerful necks with short, stiff manes. Plains zebras stand about 4 1/2 feet (1.4 m) tall at the shoulder, and weigh between 600 and 700 pounds (272.2 to 317.6 kg). Males, called stallions, are usually larger and more muscular than females, called mares.

Plains zebras have strong legs. Their hooves are made of a tough, flexible substance called keratin. Keratin is the same material found in the horns, hair, and claws of other animals.

Zebras have short, stiff manes.

Their tough hooves allow zebras to run for long distances over hard, uneven grasslands without getting sore feet. Zebras can run up to 37 miles (59.5 km) per hour. This enables them to outrun their main predators, lions and hyenas.

Zebras rely on their excellent eyesight to spot danger. They have large eyes that are set high on either side of their heads. Because of the placement of their eyes, zebras are able to watch out for predators without having to lift their heads as they graze.

Good hearing and a keen sense of smell are important to zebras. These senses help them locate predators. If a zebra feels threatened, it makes a barking noise that sounds like "kwah kwah." This call warns other zebras—and even nearby animals such as antelope and wildebeests—of approaching danger.

Zebras have excellent vision.

Grevy's Zebra

The Grevy's zebra (Equus greyvi) is the largest of the 3 species. It stands about 5 feet (1.5 m) tall at the shoulder and weighs between 750 and 950 pounds (340.2 to 431 kg). It has many narrow, closely spaced stripes that go all the way down to its hooves. A zebra's belly is pure white. These zebras have large, rounded ears, and make a noise similar to the bray of a donkey. Grevy's zebras form family and bachelor groups. These groups do not migrate long distances. Instead, they establish territories. Grevy's zebras live in the African countries of Kenya, Somalia, Ethiopia, and Sudan.

Grevy's zebras are the largest of the 3 species.

Mountain Zebras

Mountain zebras (Equus zebra) are small. They are only about 4 feet (1.2 m) tall, and weigh less than 600 pounds (272.2 kg). They have short legs and stocky bodies. Mountain zebras have wider and fewer stripes than Grevy's and plains zebras. Their ears are long and pointed like a donkey's. Mountain zebra hooves are small and narrow. This helps them move across the rocky hills and mountains where they live. They are found at elevations up to 6,500 feet (1,981 m). Like plains and Grevy's zebras, they form family and bachelor groups. Mountain zebras do not establish territories. Instead, they wander hillsides in search of water holes and grass. Mountain zebras live in South Africa, Namibia, and Angola.

Mountain zebras have wider stripes than Grevy's and plains zebras.

Special Features

A zebra's most noticeable feature is its striped coat. Its coat consists of smooth, short hair with black and white stripes. The stripes meet below its belly and continue down its legs. Each zebra has its own unique markings. Scientists believe that the stripes help in a zebra's defense. Uneven spacing of the stripes makes the edge of a zebra's shape hard to see. To a predator, a running herd of zebras looks like a solid wall of stripes. This makes it hard for the predator to tell where each animal begins and ends.

This page: Each zebra has its own special markings. **Right:** Zebra's stripes make it difficult for predators to tell where one animal begins and ends.

Social Life

Zebras often form herds of more than 500 animals. Within these large herds are smaller family groups. These consist of 6 or more mares, their offspring, and a stallion. He leads the group. Mares stay within the same family group for life. But some stallions join all-male groups, called bachelor groups. These groups are made up of males that are too young, old, or weak to lead their own group.

Herds spend most of their time feeding together during the day. Zebras are social animals. Zebras may rest their heads on another zebra's back and take a short nap. They also groom one another. They use their teeth to remove dust, dry skin, and insects from each other's coats. Grooming is an important social behavior. It helps zebras to form strong bonds with members of their group.

At night, family groups of mares and their offspring lie down to sleep. The stallion stays awake to protect the family group. If a predator approaches, the stallion will call out to wake the members of his group.

Zebras spend most of their day eating together.

Feeding

Zebras are herbivores, or plant eaters. They graze on grasses and other plants. If grass is hard to find, zebras may use their hooves to dig up juicy roots. Grass is not very nutritious or easy to digest, so zebras must feed for long periods of time to get enough to eat. They feed between 10 and 16 hours a day!

Sharp teeth are important to zebras' survival. Zebras bite off blades of grass with their front teeth. Then, they grind up the tough grass with their large flat molars. These teeth continue to grow throughout a zebra's life. This way, all the grinding a zebra does won't wear their teeth out.

Spring and summer are the rainy seasons in Africa. During these seasons,

Zebras eat grasses and other plants.

Zebras must drink water every day.

there are many water holes and fresh, green grass on the open plains. Zebras will stay where there is plenty of grass to eat. Because they need to drink water every day, zebras rarely wander far from water holes.

During the dry season, the water holes dry up and the grass turns brown. At these times, zebras must sometimes travel more than 1,000 miles (1,069 km) to find enough to eat and drink. This is dangerous for zebras because predators follow the moving herds closely. Predators may attack zebras that fall behind the herd.

The Mating Game

Mares squeal or make a whinnying noise when they are ready to mate. When stallions from nearby bachelor groups hear these noises, they approach the family group. They attempt to mate with its mares. The stallion that leads the family group tries to prevent this.

If the bachelors do not retreat, the lead stallion of the family group will fight them. When stallions fight, they paw the ground, snort, and scream. They slam into each other with their bodies. They bite each other and use their sharp hooves to strike one another. Once the loser retreats, the winner has a chance to mate with the female. The winning stallion becomes the group's new leader.

The strongest stallions are the only ones to mate. This improves the overall fitness of the herd. Some stallions may never get the chance to mate or to lead a family group.

Stallion's fight for the chance to mate with a mare.

Raising Young

Mares give birth every 2 or 3 years until they are about 24 years old. A mare is pregnant for 12 to 13 months. She usually gives birth lying down, to one baby, called a foal. Foals weigh between 55 and 70 pounds (25 to 31.8 kg) when they are born. They stand about 3 feet (1 m) tall. Their stripes are a light chocolate-brown color. Their fur is soft and fuzzy, rather than smooth like an adult zebra's. Male foals are called colts, and female foals are called fillies.

A mother cleans her newborn foal by licking it. This helps to increase the foal's circulation. It also removes birth smells that might attract predators. Foals are able to stand on their own less than an hour after they are born.

Top: Foals have brown stripes when they are born. **Bottom:** Foals drink only their mother's milk for the first few weeks after being born.

Instinctively, they follow the first moving object they see, which is usually their mother.

The mare and her foal stay away from the rest of the herd for about 3 days. If curious zebras approach, the mother chases them away. Scientists believe that this time together allows the foal to memorize its mother's smell, and possibly her stripe pattern.

Foals only drink their mother's milk during their first few weeks of life. Zebra milk helps foals quickly gain the strength they need to keep up with the rest of the herd. Within a few weeks, foals begin to eat green grasses. Eventually, they will eat only grass and plants.

Foals must have enough strength to keep up with the herd.

When foals are 4 months old, they no longer spend every moment with their mothers. Foals play together, push, and play fight. These games help young zebras improve their coordination.

Young zebras must learn to stay close to the herd for protection. Zebras are a main food source for lions. Hungry lions hide in the tall grass. They wait for a zebra herd to come near. If a young zebra wanders away from the herd, the lion will jump on it.

Fillies stay with the herd into which they were born. Colts remain with the herd until they are 3 years old. At this time, colts leave the family group to join a bachelor group. By then, their mothers usually have new foals to care for.

Young zebras stay with the herd for safety.

Zebras and Humans

In the third century, Romans captured zebras. They put them in zoos, and trained them to pull special carts, called chariots. Zebras can be ill-tempered and difficult to train. Still, European settlers in Africa used them to work on farms. For hundreds of years, African people have hunted zebras for food. People also use zebra skins to make leather.

Today, the spread of agriculture in Africa is a main threat to zebras. Grasslands are often destroyed to make room for farms. Sometimes, farmers kill zebras so that domestic livestock, such as goats and cattle, can graze on the land instead.

Conservation groups and local African governments try to preserve the zebras' habitat. Serengeti National Park was set aside to protect the large savanna area where zebras live. Tourists pay expensive park fees to watch herds of zebras race across these protected grasslands. Many local Africans earn a living as park rangers and tour guides. By working together, humans can ensure that zebras live peacefully in their natural habitats.

Plains Zebra Facts

Scientific Name: Equus burchelli

Shoulder Height: 4.5 feet tall (1.4 m)

Body Length: 5–6 feet from head to tail (1.5–1.8 m)

Weight: Weigh between 600–700 pounds (272.2–317.5 kg)

Color: Black and white stripes

Reaches sexual maturity at: Females at 13 months, males between 3 and 5 years

Gestation (pregnancy period): 12–13 months

Litter Size: Usually one foal at a time

Favorite Food: Grass

Range: Eastern and Southern Africa

Glossary

Foal A baby zebra. A male is called a colt and a female is called a filly.

Groom To clean oneself or another.

Herbivore An animal that only feeds on plants.

Herd A group of similar animals.

Migrate To travel long distances, usually in search of food and water.

Molars The back teeth used for grinding food.

Predators Animals that hunt other animals for food—for example, lions and hyenas are predators of zebras.

Further Reading

Books

Arnold, Caroline. *Zebras*. New York: William Morrow and Co., 1987.

Markert, Jenny. *Zebras*. Detroit: The Child's World, 1992.

Hoffman, Mary. *Animals in the Wild, Zebra*. London: Raintree Steck-Vaughn, 1985.

Web sites

Mountain Zebras

http://www.kidsplanet.org/factsheets/zebra.html

Zebras

http://www.imh.org/imh/bw/zebra.html

Index